An Executive's Guide to Managing Email

A must-read for any busy executive who needs to understand email marketing but not manage it day-to-day.

Wendy Hurwitz

FastFoward Publishing

Introduction

This book is designed for busy executives and senior business leaders to gain practical email operations knowledge without investing the time it takes to become an expert. In less than an hour, it will teach you how to assess and evaluate how email impacts your bottom line. You'll be able to ask the right diagnostic questions of your team to make sure your business is using email to its fullest potential. Inside you'll find:

- A practical guide to CAN-SPAM compliance
- Vendor-selection checklists
- Quick reference links

Table of Contents

The Value of Email

Busy executives often measure the health of their organization's email efforts by the sheer size of their email list. If it appears to be sizable and growing, they don't ask too many questions and accept that the program is running fine. We'll discuss it more in section 5, but list size alone is an unreliable measure of an email program's health. Size doesn't tell you when the email addresses were collected, how they were collected, if they're being used … or used properly. Size doesn't tell you if customers open your email or if they forward it to friends.

Let's begin with the topic of list health, which is often called list hygiene. List hygiene is a discipline honed over time, not a one-time effort. Think about it. If an email database has been collected over many years, a chunk of those addresses may be invalid. How often is every address used? Are the results of each send reviewed? Does someone look at inactive addresses over time? The presence of an email address on a business record does not mean it is valid. The lifespan of an email address varies by industry, but some estimates say nearly one in five adults creates an email every six months! Other estimates say a consumer email address may be good for two years, but even that isn't very long. List health requires constant monitoring, but it doesn't have to take a lot of time or effort if you know what metrics to watch.

Another reason business leaders often overlook the discipline of email list management is that it is an inexpensive sales channel. Even factoring in acquisition and production costs, email is generally cheaper to deploy than direct mail and other traditional advertising methods such as newspapers, magazines or television. As a result, managers often think sending an email, and another, and another, to promote a new product or service has a negligible cost. While it's true on the surface (the hard cost), email marketing is a bit of an iceberg. It's what you don't see that can hurt you.

Email Service Providers

To ESP or not to ESP? In the email world, an ESP is an email service provider, such as Constant Contact, ExactTarget or Cheetah Mail. There are hundreds of reputable companies who offer email services (See *Reference Worksheet* for suggested selection criteria). This section will help you decide whether or not you need an email service provider. Before you think "service provider" is merely a consulting service, let's look briefly at how emails are sent. Understanding the complexity of the process is important perspective to have as you consider this choice.

Oversimplified, when you send an email, the message travels through a network of servers connected to the internet. Each server is connected to the internet with an address, known as an IP, or internet protocol. This is a numeric string that tells the servers where to route email. Your email program – maybe Outlook as an example – connects to an SMTP (simple mail transfer protocol) server which routes your email through a network of other servers to the recipient.

Along the way, the recipient's email gets parsed such that the domain, say hotmail.com, is associated with a set of IP addresses so the email makes it to the correct destination (See resources for more web links to read up on how this works). This is much like the United States Postal Service uses a zip code, for example, to get a rough sort on where mail is headed. Zip code values start low in the Northeast part of the United States and grow larger working west, toward Alaska.

If you use an ESP, your contracted email will be routed through that company's servers. The physical routing is similar, but you're paying for both the email sends and varying-sized support teams to help navigate issues that often surface as sends occur. Do you need that assistance? I believe you do in most instances. A few items to consider:

- Evaluate your email dependency – What portion of your company's revenue is driven by email? If email as a sales channel were to disappear for a week, would it impact your bottom line?

- Staffing – How many people can you dedicate to resolving a sudden email sending issue? To monitoring day-to-day email operations? Does your staff have the skills to resolve these issues?

- Volume – How much promotional email do you send each week? Each month? A few hundred commercial emails a day poses minimal risk. Tens of thousands a day increases risk exponentially.

- List – When you send messages, are you sending to existing customers or prospects? Prospects, depending on the source/s and age of your email addresses, also pose risks.

I'm firmly in the camp of using an ESP, and believe that there are enough vendor choices to find a price point and level of service that works with organizations of all sizes.

Deliverability

What is deliverability? The simplest definition is the ability to get an email to a recipient's inbox. Engagement, SPAM traps, blacklisting, bad/invalid addresses and authentication are all components that impact deliverability. Let's take a brief look at each.

Engagement – Email engagement is determined by interactions with the messages you send. Email opens and clicks are essentially all that count. Purchases, store visits or event attendance, while a great measure of business engagement, don't count a lick when it comes to email engagement. Internet Service Providers (ISPs), such as Gmail and Yahoo, are recording your opens and clicks and translating that data into engagement metrics. A user who fails to open your email over a period of several months, may trigger their ISP to relegate your mail to a junk or bulk folder.

If you're practicing good email hygiene, you'll study the behavior of your list. From an email health perspective, *how* you segment your list is less important that what you *do* with unengaged customers. Common segments might be basic, with groups such as "click frequently," "click occasionally" and "never click," or more complex, such as clicks by message type and frequency.

The unengaged addresses are the ones you need an immediate plan for. Determine first if there is in fact a person associated with the email address. Do you see a purchase or email open associated with the address? Is the source of that email address reliable? If the answer is yes, this group of addresses could have some win-back potential. If however, there's been no measurable activity since the address was collected – and the address is more than 180 days old – proceed with caution! Old email addresses with no activity generally have the greatest likelihood of reputation damage. You might, in very small groups, starting from the most recently collected addresses, test a win-back campaign. If you start to see bounces or undeliverable messages, consider removing those – and all older email addresses – from your database. As mentioned previously, the quality of the list has more impact on your business than size.

SPAM Traps – There are two primary categories of SPAM traps, what I'll call malicious traps and recycled traps. As an email sender, you don't want either kind of trap on your list. Most ISPs give you a little latitude for the existence of traps, but good list hygiene practices are a must for businesses dependent on email-generated revenue. Intentional or malicious traps can be honey pots (i.e., email addresses created by monitoring services to catch illegal sending) or a variety of other kinds designed to catch list owners with poor hygiene practices (see *Resources* for more links). Recycled SPAM traps are generally used by ISPs to monitor good sending practices. An ISP for example, may "repurpose" an email address after 180 days of no activity. If senders continue to hit that address, the ISP knows they're not practicing good hygiene practices.

IP health – Earlier in the book we discussed IP addresses, so you know what they are and how they function in sending email from one computer to another. These addresses develop reputations over time, reflecting the quality of the data being transmitted.
Reputation – The cumulative track record of an IP address over time. Note that even corrected bad practices, or recovery from a single bad slip may take more than a month of continued "good behavior" to resolve.

CAN-SPAM – This abbreviation stands for Controlling the Assault of Non-Solicited Pornography and Marketing Act of 2003. Passed in 2004, the act essentially defines commercial email and describes sending rules that most legitimate senders would follow anyway. These include things like making subject lines clear and accurate, identifying the email sender and their physical location and allowing recipients to opt-out of receiving commercial messages. What kinds of messages are classified as commercial? These include, but are not limited to, advertisements and promotions, including press releases and new product announcements. If your message applies to a group – of businesses or consumers – it is likely commercial. If you have any doubt, consult an attorney.

For those of you using third-parties to manage your email sends, know that the law holds you responsible for what that company/service/agency is doing. Check the resources section for additional details on CAN-SPAM compliance.

If you have any recipients in Canada, you must also comply with CASL, the Canadian Anti-Spam Legislation. This is markedly different than the U.S. law – especially with regard to consent and previously existing business relationships – so take care to bone up on what's needed to be compliant. Start with an examination of your databases. Do you have .ca email addresses? If not, double-check your mailing addresses as well for Canadian addresses. Even if your address collection form doesn't accept a country choice other than the U.S., you may find entries in your database that circumvent the form. I've seen a few brands *think* they're blocking international addresses, only to find Canadian city and zip data paired with random state selections in their databases. If you do have Canadian addresses in your database, or known users in the country, you want to have an attorney review your opt-in practices for compliance.

Note that the previous discussion is limited to commercial messages. Many other emails from a business to a consumer are called transactional emails. These are non-promotional, non-advertising emails. Examples of transactional emails would be purchase confirmations and statement of accounts. The primary purpose of the email is about an interaction that has taken place (perhaps an order) and is not soliciting a new purchase (note too, that new product announcements, name/brand changes and renewal messaging are generally considered to be commercial, not transactional messages). While not required, it is advisable to have an opt-out option included (at least in the footer) of transactional emails. The typical customer doesn't differentiate between commercial and transactional emails and will expect to see this option in every message from reputable companies.

Good email practices are really good marketing practices. You're applying the same basic segmentation and messaging principles to your email list.

Testing

Email testing should be a critical part of any marketing program, regardless of how much or how little volume you send. Let's say your business sends only transactional email. Perhaps your standard email sends include only purchase confirmations or receipts. Isn't it in your best interest to make sure these messages are seen by as many customers as possible?

If these billing or shipping statements also include promotional messaging, you probably want to see which product or information pairings work best. The other extreme is an ecommerce business that relies on email to generate a large portion of site traffic and/or sales. These businesses depend on testing – it can truly make the difference between success and failure.

Common tests

Send time – The time of day you send email may or may not make a big difference in sales. I've seen big variations by industry (see *Resources* for link), and of course, what the call to action is in the email messaging. If you're going to experiment, start small and benchmark results. If you typically deploy your email at 8 a.m. local time, make your next test 7:30 or 9 a.m., not noon. Only after small, incremental changes show little impact should you consider a radical time change. Then, use a small percentage of your list as a test group before moving the entire list to a new send time. Consider other factors such as the opening of your stores and/or call centers to make sure they're aligned. If your customer service center doesn't open until 8 a.m., your first test might be better deployed at 9 a.m. to minimize any spike in calls to an unattended line.

Consider as well the percentage of mobile traffic you get to your site. If your customers/clients are accessing your site on mobile devices, you'll likely see more variation in "drive time" experiments than you will by sending at lunch time. If you're targeting government workers, you might want to stay within a more traditional 9 a.m. to 5 p.m. timeframe. This test is important even to the most traditional of companies. So much of web traffic has shifted from desktop to mobile in the last several years, it's strongly recommended that you monitor device and browser traffic no less than quarterly. As you begin to see your site's user behavior change, it only makes sense to begin shifting your thinking on how you deliver your product offerings.

Subject line – This is the fastest way to see powerful impact on email performance. The subject line drives whether or not the recipient opens an email, so it makes sense that subtle changes can make a huge difference. Keep in mind that subject line testing is also an ongoing effort. What works today may or may not continue to work three to six months from now. Many ESPs maintain a list of trigger words to avoid using in your subject lines (see *Resources* for a partial list). Experts will argue this list to some extent, but it's safest to use their suggestions until you have a reliably performing control.

Frequency – To what extent does send frequency impact purchase or click behavior for your business? You'll have to experiment to find out. You may find that different customer segments have radically different tolerances for messages about your products and services. This could change with content, so be sure to note the offer when evaluating the performance as a whole. You could have a segment of buyers who will respond to almost every discount offer, but would unsubscribe if you sent informational emails with the same frequency.

Creative testing – Once your subject lines are perfected, your team should move on to creative tests, which include everything from how the call to action (CTA) is stated, what images are used, and even the color of the click-through buttons.

There's also the issue of mobile optimized and responsive design. While an entire book could be written on this subject alone, first look at the business you're in and how consumers interact with your site.

If you're not selling something or providing an on-the-go directory of reference resource, there may be less mobile consumption. In that case, you can probably create a mobile friendly email and be fine. This might be a one-column format with large buttons that make it easy for navigation on a small smart phone screen. If however, your customers need to buy a product or service, you'll want to consider responsive design. This design technology allows the email to resize automatically by device. It improves the user experience significantly but takes more time (and generally expense) to produce.

Assessments

Click-through rate (CTR) – If the subject line is the bait you cast to get an open, the CTR measures the worthiness of the actual content. Testing one thing at a time, you can quickly iterate a stronger control email. Remember to change only one thing at a time so you know what drives the change. I've seen a surprising lift from changes made to button color (e.g., "Click Here") or call to action text (e.g., "Manage Subscription" versus "Access Your Account."

If you don't have an ESP where you can readily access all test data in one spot, keep a spreadsheet of your efforts. A basic data set might look like this:

Date	Subject Line	Content	Sent	Open Rte	Click Rte	Unsub	Unsub Rte*
2/13/15	Sweet Treat on us: 50% all Valentine's Day orders!	Holiday Discount Sales	40,200	9.9%	1.8%	211	0.5%
2/13/15	Sweet Treat on us: All Valentine's Day orders discounted!	Holiday Discount Sales	40,196	8.4%	1.5%	100	0.3%
2/13/15	50% off all Valentine's Day orders!	Holiday Discount Sales	40,210	10.1%	1.9%	150	0.4%

See page 14 for a larger representation of this data set

Note: ESPs vary on their calculations, but we recommend evaluating unsubscribe rates based on emails delivered, not sent

Date	Subject Line	Content	Sent	Open Rte	Click Rte	Unsub	Unsub Rte*
2/13/15	Sweet Treat on us: 50% all Valentine's Day orders!	Holiday Discount Sales	40,200	9.9%	1.7%	211	0.5%
2/13/15	Sweet Treat on us: All Valentine's Day orders discounted!	Holiday Discount Sales	40,196	8.4%	1.5%	100	0.3%
2/13/15	50% off all Valentine's Day orders!	Holiday Discount Sales	40,210	10.1%	1.9%	150	0.4%

*Note: ESPs vary on their calculations, but we recommend evaluating unsubscribe rates based on emails delivered, not sent

Unsubscribe Activity – With each test executed, record the unsubscribe activity and the number of SPAM complaints received. This gives you a well-rounded picture of what information customers expect from email. A terrific subject line may beat your control on open rate, but if recipients don't like the message inside, it could share a very high unsubscribe rate. Judge success on how well these run in synch. Unsubscribe rates vary by industry, and by type of message (i.e., commercial versus transactional) so once you find an appropriate range, consider carefully any messaging that takes you too far off course.

Finally, if you're not tracking conversion of your emails with marketing automation software or some kind of tracking software, make sure all emails have UTM parameters in the email links. Then you can use the free version of Google Analytics (there's a six-figure paid version as well). When properly configured by your tech team, the tool gives you a real-time view of email performance (conversion).

List Building Techniques

There are several ways for a business to grow their email lists, paid and organic. We'll look at each separately.

Paid techniques are probably the fastest way to grow lists, but arguably riskier. Examples include rented or purchased lists, co-registration, digital display ads and affiliate marketing. If you've been in business for any length of time, you've likely received solicitation emails offering lists for rental or purchase for unbelievably low prices. While there are some credible vendors out there, purchasing email addresses is generally a bad idea. There are several reasons. First, attrition will be higher than a home-grown list. If recipients didn't explicitly provide you with their email address, the chances that they'll respond favorably to any kind of offer is unlikely. Second, their overall lifetime value and average order value are likely to be lower. Generally rental lists are compiled from people who have made purchases in a similar category – or who share demographic attributes of people who buy or behave like your target – so it's a leap of faith that they need your specific product/service. Third, if you don't know how the vendor collected the email addresses they're making available to you, you could be opening the door to a lot of customer service issues.

Two credible means of email list growth are paid media (i.e., display, SEO, PPC) and affiliate marketing (also paid, but generally available through a network rather than a direct purchase). Picking the right channels (paid) and partners (affiliate) depends a lot on your business segment and budget. My general rule of thumb is to pay for external expertise when you can, and have an internal staffer manage the performance of those vendors. This way you can grow or contract your level of spend on performance and not invest in full-time staff until you're ready.

Paid acquisition is really just digital media buying, rather than the "media buying" that used to include just broadcast, print and outdoor (OOH). There are a number of legitimate ways to place media, but first consider your risk tolerance, expectations and budget.

Casting a large net at a lower relative cost – say, buying based on impressions – may make sense if your goal is to get your brand's name out with no specific call to action. It might not make sense however, if your goal is immediate conversion, where you'd trade a higher cost for completed transactions. In that case, a CPA (cost per acquisition, usually a completed transaction) or CPL (cost per lead, usually an email address or contact information) campaign might make more sense. Finding publishers (the name given to websites that host ad content) who will share risk (e.g., CPA rather than CPM) may require the help of an agency or affiliate network.

Co-registration, where your opt-in offer will likely appear with others after a completed transaction on another web site, is pretty low risk with fair performance. The better networks will provide sample publishers in their networks so you can pick and choose which tiers make sense for your products and your brands. Beware of gaming or other sites that use incentives to garner opt-in actions for their co-registration partners. The addresses/date you get are likely to churn and have limited lifetime value.

Organic growth comes from normal, mostly unpaid business practices. Word-of-mouth, web forms and referrals are all types of organic traffic. "Hand raisers" that register/request information/subscribe on their own are generally better, long-term customers. With the exception of brand new businesses – that may need to increase awareness to customers of all kinds – folks who come to you on their own generally have higher average order value (AOV) and lifetime value (LTV).

Common organic techniques include member-get-a-member programs and self-promotion on a company website, in email or at a company-hosted event (or any other type of owned and operated media channel). Others use point-of-purchase material, from point-of-sale and window clings to store signage and on--receipt messaging.

IP Warming - While most businesses many not do enough email volume to warrant dozens of IP addresses (one IP address with a good reputation can typically carry daily volume in the millions), there are a variety of reasons you may wish to spread your sending over at least a couple.

If something were to go wrong with one, say a deliverability problem with one ISP, you could re-direct sends to a secondary IP. You might want to segment your list by engagement behaviors and spread the groups over different IPs. New IP addresses must be "warmed" over time — usually over a couple of months or so — so that you don't look like a spammer (sudden spike in volume from a previously unknown IP address). This is another reason an ESP is a good idea, as they can help you load balance sending to slowly increase sending by ISP until you're at maintenance levels. With some ISPs being very sensitive, you may only be able to send about 5k per day at the outset to prevent problems. Plan ahead! Don't let a critical campaign get derailed because of IP warming.

Reference Worksheet
Choosing an Email Service Provider (ESP)

As you consider several email service providers, I suggest you create some kind of scoring mechanism whereby you apply the same set of criteria to each vendor. Make a list of considerations (a partial list is included in the chart below), determine how important each one is (weight each from 1 to 5, with 5 being the bests score) and rate each vendor. After you've done your research, the final candidates will be those with the highest scores. I'd strongly suggest asking for – and actually calling – several references. Ask for those who work in similar industries and/or similarly-sized companies.

Variable	Weight	Rating (1-5)	Vendor A	Vendor B
Dedicated or low-share IP				
Training				
CAN-SPAM compliance				
Reporting				
List management				
Testing				
Support				
Free trial				
Overall cost				
Implementation speed				
Third-party ecosystem				
Other_____				
Other_____				

See page 20 for a larger representation of vendor consideration criteria

Dedicated IP – As we discussed previously, a shared IP address makes sense if you're just starting out and don't have significant revenue dependency on email. Your email would share a pipe, so to speak, with that of other businesses. Benefits include reduced costs and no IP warm-up time. IPs function best when carrying hundreds of thousands of emails per month, so a small- or mid-sized business may never have enough volume to warrant a standalone address. The drawbacks of course, are related to sharing. If a partner sends to a bad email list, the shared IP could get blacklisted and be inaccessible to your business for some time. The cost of a dedicated IP may not be where you want to invest if you're running minimal volume.

Variable	Weight	Rating (1-5)	Vendor A	Vendor B
Dedicated or low-share IP				
Training				
CAN-SPAM compliance				
Reporting				
List management				
Testing				
Support				
Free trial				
Overall cost				
Implementation speed				
Third-party ecosystem				
Other____				
Other____				

Training – Whether you have one user or a dozen, you'll want an ESP with some kind of training support. If your contract includes a fixed block of hours, you'll want to negotiate in advance for additional support hours that may come along later. Ask about previously recorded training sessions that might be free, as well as online help features.

CAN-SPAM – To protect yourself (and your company), it's better to err on the conservative side and choose a vendor who will force CAN-SPAM compliance in their email tools. One slip could be very costly.

Reporting – Decide in advance what kinds of metrics you'll need to evaluate your email campaigns. Then ask to see how reports are generated and whether or not you can use the output "as-is" in your organization.

List management – While every ESP will have rudimentary list management tools, you may find that segmentation tools are helpful. If you have a large database team, this may be less of a consideration.

Testing capacity – At the least, you may want to consider a tool with A/B test capabilities. Simply, this allows you to run a test with two groups at the same time. Most small companies don't need multivariate testing, but some ESPs have plug-ins to make this possible.

Support – Whether it's on-boarding a new employee or resolving an ISP block, know what you have access to in advance. Again, negotiate additional support hours at a fixed rate in advance of needing them. Understand how quickly different support requests will be addressed with very detailed SLAs. Note too, that the level of support will vary greatly between an enterprise ESP and one that's available with a low, monthly credit card payment.

Free trial – Most vendors will give you a free trial period or rebate your trial fee when you sign a contract. This is a great way to get hands-on experience with a tool, its functionality and ease of use.

Overall cost – Most ESPs will charge based on volume. To the extent that you can, give yourself a little cushion in the initial volume estimate and again, negotiate additional (volume) blocks in advance.

Some ESPs will allow you to renew early – at higher volume – and apply the new negotiated rate backward to cover an overage. Be creative!

Implementation Speed – An enterprise ESP will probably have a large services organization that can implement on an accelerated schedule. A smaller, online only ESP may require a several-week wait to get you started. Understand the timeline from contract execution to 'first send' before you choose a partner.

Third-party Ecosystem – The larger ESPs have numerous third-party partners with adjacent software and services capabilities. If you need to connect your email software to other sales tools, ask prospective ESPs if and how their tools connect.

Reference - Words that May Trigger SPAM Traps

This list is a fluid list gathered from a number of email service providers and SPAM authorities, such as SpamAssassin, Return Path and eConsultancy. While there are very few words that alone will cause problems, it's a best practice to avoid these:

> FREE, 100% free, F R E E
> Make $, Save $
> No gimmicks
> Urgent
> Please Read
> Donate
> Money-Back Guarantee
> Apply now
> Opportunity
> Weight loss

I'd also recommend avoiding subject lines in ALL CAPS (suggests the voice equivalent of screaming), and judicious use of dingbats (picture icons – they don't render on all devices or email clients).

Reference - Online Resources

Research Resources

> eMarketer – Sign up for their free newsletters, which often include industry-specific benchmarking reports. Both paid and free resources are offered. http://www.emarketer.com/

> Marketing Sherpa – A MECLABs company, Marketing Sherpa is a huge repository of case studies, research reports and other resources. Both paid and free resources are offered. http://www.marketingsherpa.com/

Legal Resources

> CAN-SPAM – This book in no way provides legal counsel. Only qualified attorneys can advise your business and interpret legislation.

> For a complete CAN-SPAM overview, I recommend these resources:
> http://www.business.ftc.gov/documents/bus61-can-spam-act-compliance-guide-business and
> http://www.gpo.gov/fdsys/pkg/PLAW-108publ187/pdf/PLAW-108publ187.pdf

> CASL – These sites are a good starting point for the corresponding Canadian anti-spam legislation:
> https://www.ic.gc.ca/eic/site/ecic-ceac.nsf/eng/gv00521.html and
> http://fightspam.gc.ca/eic/site/030.nsf/eng/home

Vendor Resources

This is not an exhaustive – or endorsed – vendor list. If you conduct a web search for "email service provider" you will find numerous vendors for your consideration. Most vendors have a specialty, so know exactly what you need before you start (the "nice to have" list could be expensive).

Cheetah Mail - http://www.experian.com/marketing-services/cheetahmail.html

Constant Contact - http://www.constantcontact.com/index.jsp They recently published helpful benchmark data on email open times by industry at http://support2.constantcontact.com/articles/FAQ/1303

eBay Enterprise (formerly eDialog) - http://www.ebayenterprise.com/marketing_solutions/email/

Mail Chimp - http://mailchimp.com/

Responsys (by Oracle) - http://www.responsys.com/email-marketing

SalesForce Marketing Cloud - http://www.exacttarget.com/products/email-marketing

Silverpop (by IBM) - http://www.silverpop.com/

StrongView - http://www.strongview.com/

YesMail - http://www.yesmail.com/

AWeber - http://www.aweber.com/start-sending.htm?gclid=CM6bjKmvy8MCFXMQ7AoduS8Atw

List Building Resources

Commission Junction - http://www.cj.com/ - A large affiliate marketing company that helps you acquire and manage a network of affiliate (site) partners who sell on your behalf. They offer DIY and managed services.

Opt-Intelligence - http://www.opt-intelligence.com/ Provides co-registration partnerships with major publishers

Testing Resources

Google Analytics - http://www.google.com/analytics/

Monetate - http://www.monetate.com/ Software that allows real-time testing and dynamic presentation/personalization of content.

Optimizely - https://www.optimizely.com/ This A/B testing software allows you to divert some portion of your site traffic to a test version of your site. As you make changes, the software enables you to see – real time – what impact the change/s have on your conversion process.

Hygiene Resources

https://wordtothewise.com/2011/08/a-brief-guide-to-spamtraps/
http://www.freshaddress.com/home.php
http://www.returnpath.com/

About the Author

Wendy Hurwitz is a marketing executive with 20+ years experience working at Fortune 500 & Fortune Global 500 companies

An Executive's Guide to Managing Email

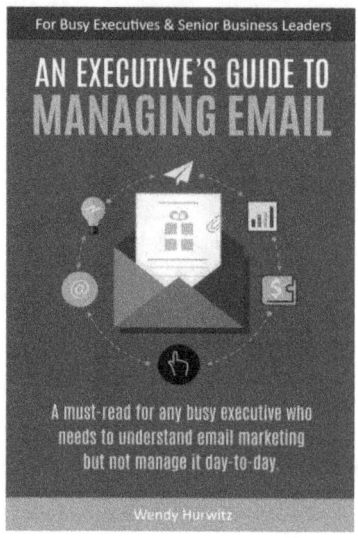

Copyright © 2015 Wendy Hurwitz

Published in the United States by FastForward Publishing